Hosted by

On This Day

Guests

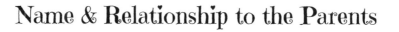

Name & Relationship to the Parents

_____

Wishes for Baby

_____
_____
_____

Any Advice?

_____
_____
_____
_____

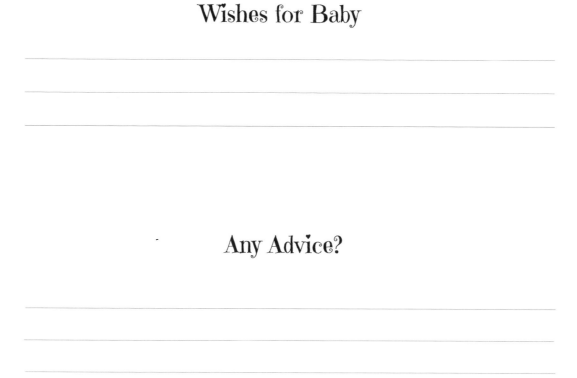

Guests

Name & Relationship to the Parents

Wishes for Baby

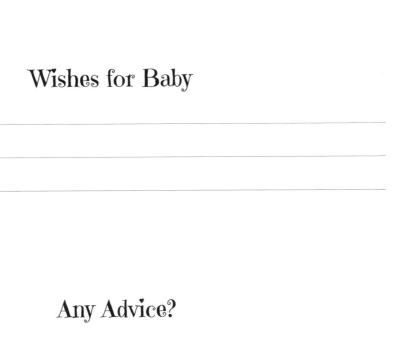

Any Advice?

Guests

Name & Relationship to the Parents

_____

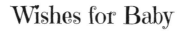

Wishes for Baby

_____

_____

_____

Any Advice?

_____

_____

_____

_____

Guests

Name & Relationship to the Parents

Wishes for Baby

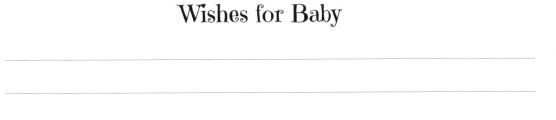

Any Advice?

Guests

Name & Relationship to the Parents

_____

Wishes for Baby

_____

_____

_____

Any Advice?

_____

_____

_____

_____

Guests

Name & Relationship to the Parents

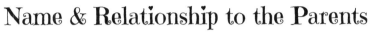

Wishes for Baby

_____

_____

_____

Any Advice?

_____

_____

_____

_____

Guests

Name & Relationship to the Parents

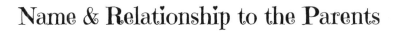

Wishes for Baby

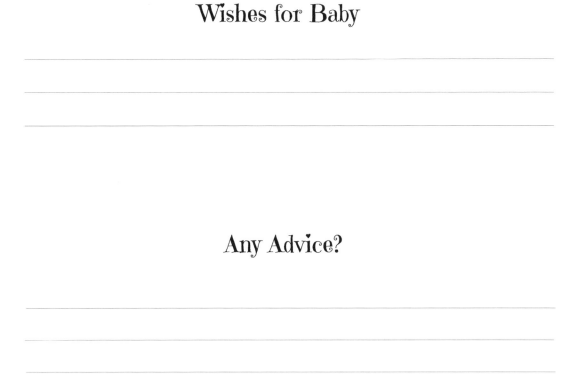

Any Advice?

Guests

Name & Relationship to the Parents

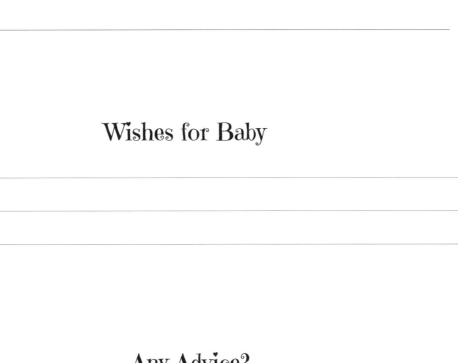

Wishes for Baby

Any Advice?

Guests

Name & Relationship to the Parents

Wishes for Baby

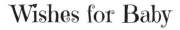

Any Advice?

Guests

Name & Relationship to the Parents

Wishes for Baby

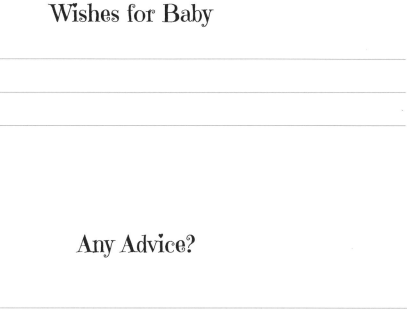

Any Advice?

Guests

Name & Relationship to the Parents

Wishes for Baby

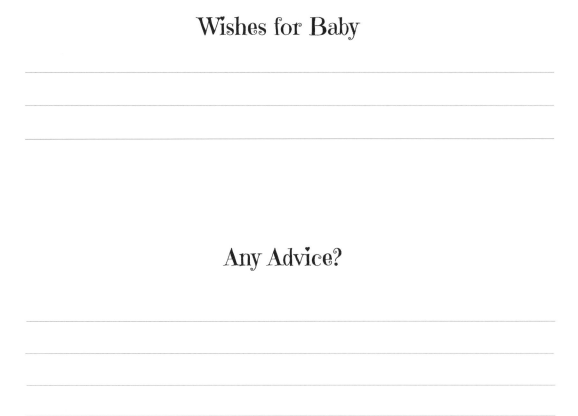

Any Advice?

Guests

Name & Relationship to the Parents

Wishes for Baby

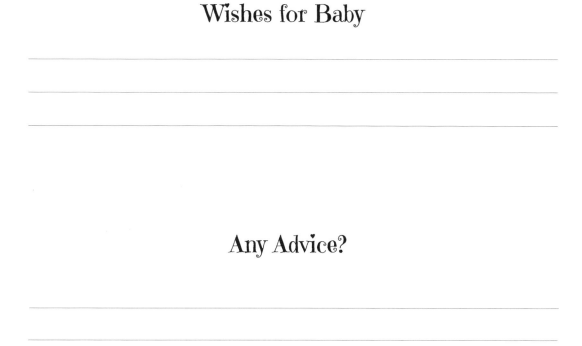

Any Advice?

Guests

Name & Relationship to the Parents

Wishes for Baby

_____

_____

_____

Any Advice?

_____

_____

_____

_____

Guests

Name & Relationship to the Parents

Wishes for Baby

_____

_____

_____

Any Advice?

_____

_____

_____

_____

Guests

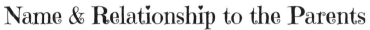

Name & Relationship to the Parents

_____

Wishes for Baby

_____

_____

_____

Any Advice?

_____

_____

_____

_____

Guests

Name & Relationship to the Parents

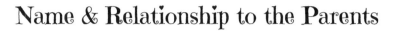

Wishes for Baby

Any Advice?

Guests

Name & Relationship to the Parents

Wishes for Baby

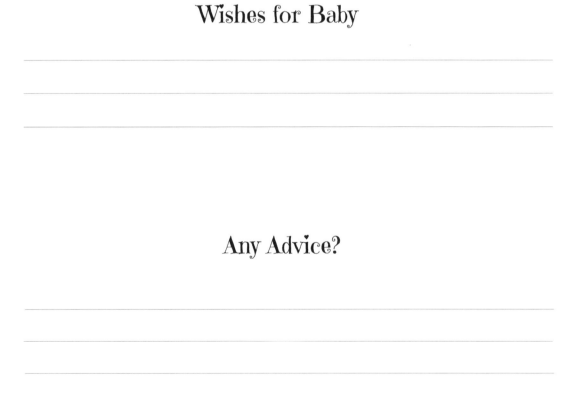

Any Advice?

Guests

Name & Relationship to the Parents

Wishes for Baby

Any Advice?

Guests

Name & Relationship to the Parents

Wishes for Baby

Any Advice?

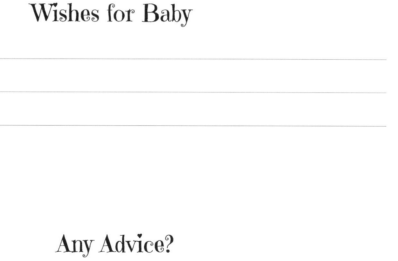

Guests

Name & Relationship to the Parents

Wishes for Baby

Any Advice?

Guests

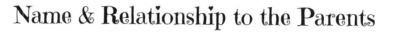

Name & Relationship to the Parents

Wishes for Baby

Any Advice?

Guests

Name & Relationship to the Parents

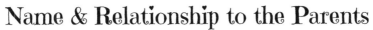

Wishes for Baby

Any Advice?

Guests

Name & Relationship to the Parents

_____

Wishes for Baby

_____
_____
_____

Any Advice?

_____
_____
_____
_____

Guests

Name & Relationship to the Parents

Wishes for Baby

Any Advice?

Guests

Name & Relationship to the Parents

Wishes for Baby

Any Advice?

Guests

Name & Relationship to the Parents

Wishes for Baby

Any Advice?

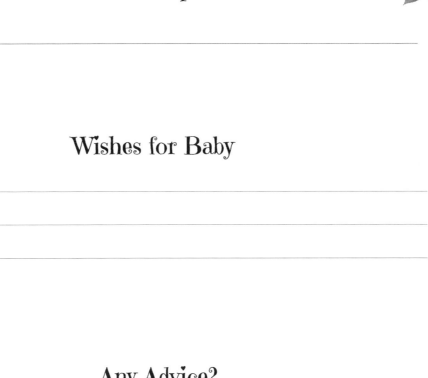

Guests

Name & Relationship to the Parents

Wishes for Baby

Any Advice?

Guests

Name & Relationship to the Parents

Wishes for Baby

Any Advice?

Guests

Name & Relationship to the Parents

Wishes for Baby

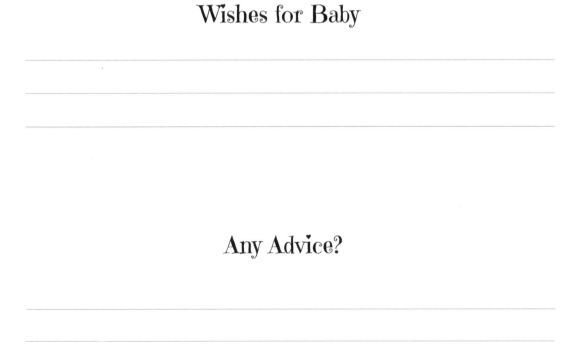

Any Advice?

Guests

Name & Relationship to the Parents

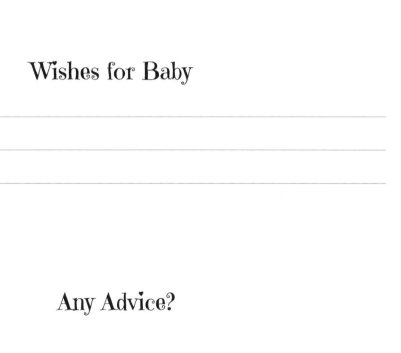

Wishes for Baby

_____

_____

_____

Any Advice?

_____

_____

_____

Guests

Name & Relationship to the Parents

Wishes for Baby

Any Advice?

Guests

Name & Relationship to the Parents

Wishes for Baby

_____

_____

_____

Any Advice?

_____

_____

_____

_____

Guests

Name & Relationship to the Parents

_____

Wishes for Baby

_____

_____

_____

Any Advice?

_____

_____

_____

_____

Guests

Name & Relationship to the Parents

Wishes for Baby

Any Advice?

Guests

Name & Relationship to the Parents

_____

Wishes for Baby

_____

_____

_____

Any Advice?

_____

_____

_____

_____

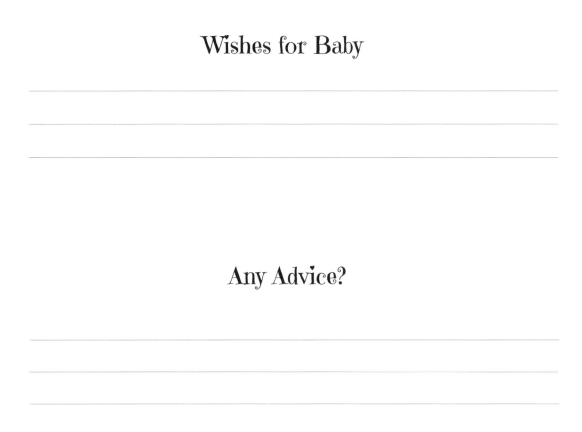

Guests

Name & Relationship to the Parents

Wishes for Baby

Any Advice?

Guests

Name & Relationship to the Parents

Wishes for Baby

Any Advice?

Guests

Name & Relationship to the Parents

Wishes for Baby

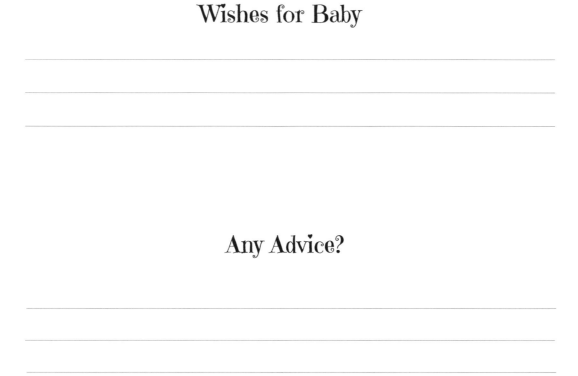

Any Advice?

Guests

Name & Relationship to the Parents

Wishes for Baby

Any Advice?

Guests

Name & Relationship to the Parents

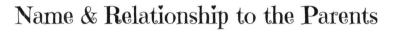

Wishes for Baby

Any Advice?

Guests

Name & Relationship to the Parents

Wishes for Baby

Any Advice?

Guests

Name & Relationship to the Parents

Wishes for Baby

Any Advice?

Guests

Name & Relationship to the Parents

Wishes for Baby

Any Advice?

Guests

Name & Relationship to the Parents

Wishes for Baby

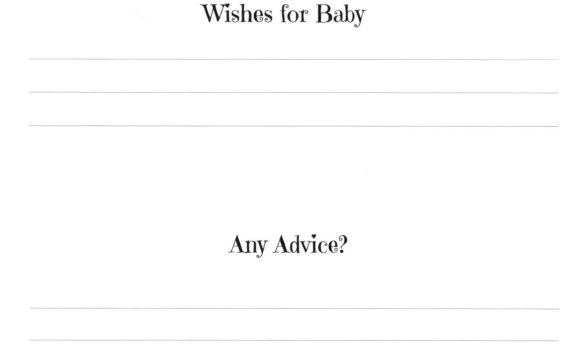

Any Advice?

Guests

Name & Relationship to the Parents

Wishes for Baby

Any Advice?

Guests

Name & Relationship to the Parents

Wishes for Baby

Any Advice?

Guests

Name & Relationship to the Parents

_____

Wishes for Baby

_____

_____

_____

Any Advice?

_____

_____

_____

_____

Guests

Name & Relationship to the Parents

_____

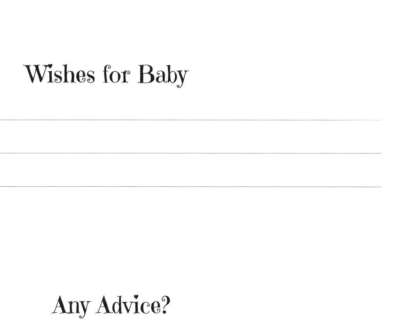

Wishes for Baby

_____
_____
_____

Any Advice?

_____
_____
_____
_____

Guests

Name & Relationship to the Parents

Wishes for Baby

Any Advice?

Guests

Name & Relationship to the Parents

Wishes for Baby

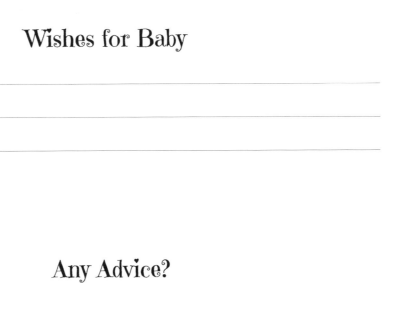

Any Advice?

Guests

Name & Relationship to the Parents

Wishes for Baby

Any Advice?

Guests

Name & Relationship to the Parents

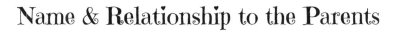

Wishes for Baby

Any Advice?

Guests

Name & Relationship to the Parents

Wishes for Baby

Any Advice?

Guests

Name & Relationship to the Parents

Wishes for Baby

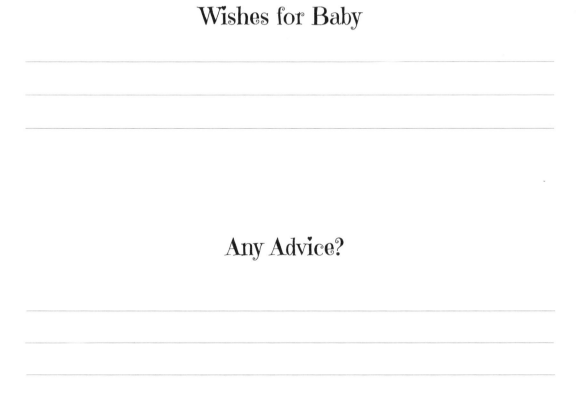

Any Advice?

Guests

Name & Relationship to the Parents

Wishes for Baby

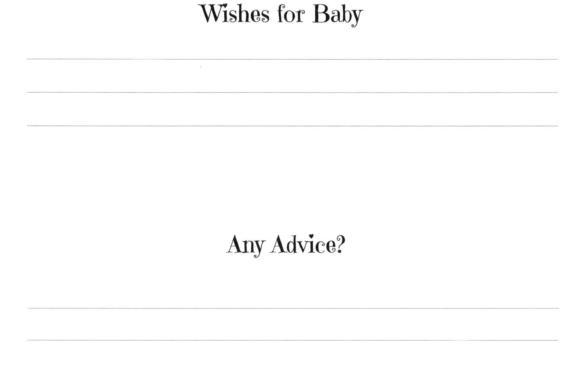

Any Advice?

Guests

Name & Relationship to the Parents

Wishes for Baby

Any Advice?

Guests

Name & Relationship to the Parents

Wishes for Baby

Any Advice?

Guests

Name & Relationship to the Parents

Wishes for Baby

Any Advice?

Guests

Name & Relationship to the Parents

Wishes for Baby

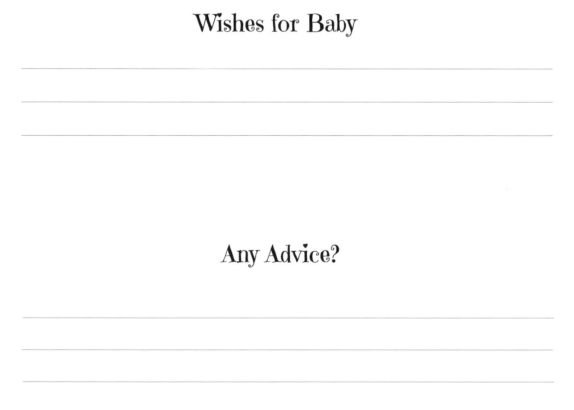

Any Advice?

Guests

Name & Relationship to the Parents

Wishes for Baby

Any Advice?

Guests

Name & Relationship to the Parents

Wishes for Baby

Any Advice?

Guests

Name & Relationship to the Parents

Wishes for Baby

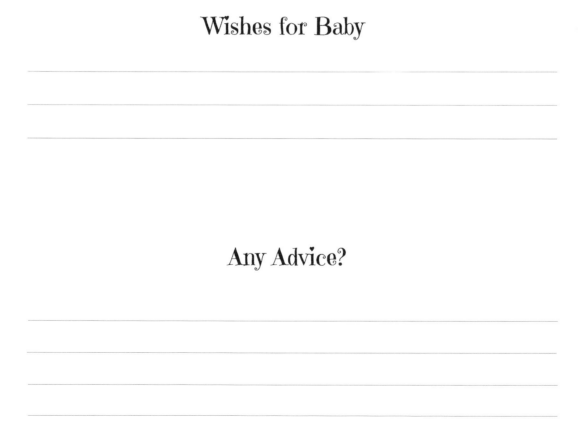

Any Advice?

Guests

Name & Relationship to the Parents

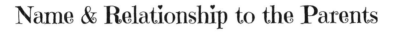

Wishes for Baby

Any Advice?

Guests

Name & Relationship to the Parents

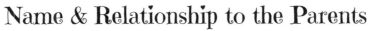

Wishes for Baby

Any Advice?

Guests

Name & Relationship to the Parents

Wishes for Baby

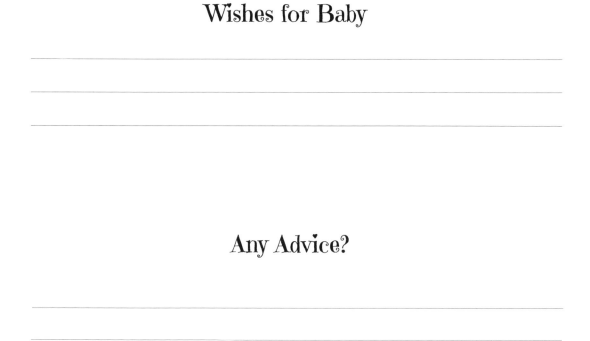

Any Advice?

Guests

Name & Relationship to the Parents

Wishes for Baby

Any Advice?

Guests

Name & Relationship to the Parents

Wishes for Baby

Any Advice?

Guests

Name & Relationship to the Parents

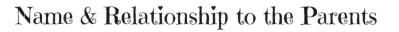

Wishes for Baby

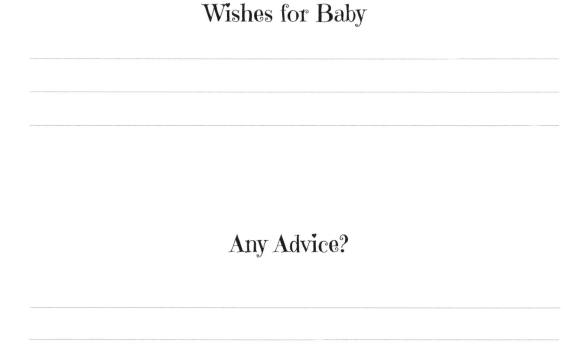

Any Advice?

Guests

Name & Relationship to the Parents

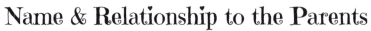

Wishes for Baby

Any Advice?

Guests

Name & Relationship to the Parents

_____

Wishes for Baby

_____

_____

_____

Any Advice?

_____

_____

_____

Guests

Name & Relationship to the Parents

Wishes for Baby

Any Advice?

Guests

Name & Relationship to the Parents

Wishes for Baby

Any Advice?

Guests

Name & Relationship to the Parents

Wishes for Baby

Any Advice?

Guests

Name & Relationship to the Parents

Wishes for Baby

Any Advice?

Guests

Name & Relationship to the Parents

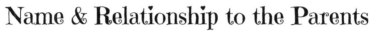

Wishes for Baby

Any Advice?

Guests

Name & Relationship to the Parents

Wishes for Baby

Any Advice?

Gift Log

Gift Received

Given By

Gift Log

Gift Received

Given By

Gift Log

Gift Received

Given By

Gift Log

Gift Received	Given By

Gift Log

Gift Received

Given By

Gift Log

Gift Received   Given By

 # Gift Log

Gift Received	Given By

Gift Log

Gift Received

Given By

Gift Log

Gift Received   Given By

 # Gift Log

Gift Received   Given By

Gift Log

Gift Received

Given By

Gift Log

Gift Received

Given By

Special Memories and Photos

Special Memories and Photos

Special Memories and Photos

Special Memories and Photos

Special Memories and Photos

Special Memories and Photos

Special Memories and Photos

Special Memories and Photos

Special Memories and Photos

Special Memories and Photos

Special Memories and Photos

Made in the USA
Las Vegas, NV
20 August 2022

53643390R00060